FOUL-MOUTH FELINES

A HUMOROUS ADULT COLORING BOOK FOR CAT LOVERS

I REALLY DON'T GIVE A RATS ASS

I DON'T ALWAYS GIVE A SHIT BUT WHEN I DO, I BURY IT.

You can Kiss my Furry Ass

Well ShiT Happens

I'm Fresh out of Fucks

I'M FLYING THIS BACKWARD-ASS SHIT SHOW

I'M SICK OF THIS SHIT

BITCH TO SOMEONE THAT ACTUALLY GIVES A FUCK

YOU NEED TO CHILL THE FUCK OUT!

Calm the Fuck down

IT IS WHAT IT FUCKING IS

Sorry Dickhead,
I'm bipolar, we good?

I'M ALLERGIC TO ALL THIS BULLSHIT

THIS IS MY DON'T GIVE A SHIT FACE

Mind your own Business
Asswipe Sniffer!

Hey Asshole, What are you smiling about?

LET THAT MOTHER FUCKIN SHIT GO

GOT NO TIME FOR YOUR BALL SLAPPING BULLSHIT

EAT A SACK OF BROKEN DICKS

I do a thing called whatever the Fuck I want

WHAT A CLUSTERFUCK

LOOK AT ME
I'M A FLYING FUCK

PRETTY FUCKIN DOPE
KEEP THAT SHIT UP

Hello, I'm sleeping
Jackass

I'VE GOT ZERO FUCKS TO GIVE

I'M A PRICK WHATS YOUR SUPERPOWER

My Shit doesn't stink

THEY'RE SOME SALTY BITCHES

WHOOPTI
FUCKING DO!

OK, NOW TELL SOMEONE WHO GIVES A CRAP